The history of emigration from
CHINA
& SOUTH-EAST ASIA

Katherine Prior

FRANKLIN WATTS
LONDON • NEW YORK • SYDNEY

First published in 1997 by Franklin Watts
96 Leonard Street, London EC2A 4RH

Franklin Watts Australia
14 Mars Road
Lane Cove
NSW 2066

Editor: Suzy Jenvey
Series editor: Rachel Cooke
Designer: Simon Borrough
Picture research: Sarah Moule

A CIP catalogue record for this book is
available from the British Library.

ISBN 0 7496 2580 5

Dewey Classification 304.80951

Printed in Malaysia

Picture acknowledgements

t=top; b=bottom; m=middle; r=right; l=left
The Anthony Blake Agency p. 19
Associated Press/Topham p. 20b
The Bridgeman Art Gallery pp. 4t, 7b, 16
Corbis-Bettmann pp. 11t, 12b
Hawaii State Archives pp. 8t, 9b, 10, 14t, 14b
Hocken Library, Otago NZ. p. 13t
Hulton Deutsch p. 11
Idaho State Historical Society p. 13b
The Image Bank pp. 4b, 5, 21b, 24b, 25t, 28b
The Mansell Collection p. 7t
The Mary Evans Picture Library pp. 9t, 12t
Panos Pictures pp. 15t (Heldur Netocny), 15b
(R. Giling), 18b (Chris Stowers), 22t (D.K.
Hulcher), 23t (P. Tweedie)
Photobank/BKK p. 26t
Magnum Photos pp. 17t (Helen Snow), 17b
(Penny Tweedie), 22b (P. Zachmann), 23b and
27t (Paul Fusco), 24t (Alex Webb), 25b (T.
Hoepker), 26b (C. Steele-Perkins)
Rex Features p. 21t
Sipa Press p. 29
The Robert Harding Picture Library pp. 6b,
18t, 20t, 28t
Map by Julian Baker

Contents

China: empire under attack

Warfare, famine and land scarcity.

The decision to emigrate is never an easy one. Whatever the dreams of a new life in a new country, leaving behind family, friends and the familiar foods and customs of one's homeland is hard. In some countries, the people's attachment to their land and culture is so strong that few ever leave. For centuries China was like that, but the warfare, famine and land scarcity of the 19th century made people desperate. More and more Chinese and people from neighbouring countries in South-East Asia made the decision to leave their homeland and seek work in foreign countries.

An ancient civilization

China is one of the world's largest countries, with a population today of over 1 billion people. It has an ancient civilization famous for technological advances. The Chinese invented paper,

▲ The Chinese developed one of the earliest forms of centralized government with the Emperor as the supreme leader.

The Ancient ▶ Chinese thought of the Emperor's palace in the Forbidden City in Peking (Beijing) as the centre of the universe.

silk, porcelain, printing and gunpowder, all of which were enthusiastically copied by Europeans.

The Chinese were proud of their civilization, but they were not ready to copy from foreigners as foreigners had copied from them. By the 18th century, China's technology lagged behind the West. As Europe embarked on the Industrial Revolution, China turned her back to the world.

The region of South-East Asia consists of a strip of mainland and thousands of islands. From the 16th to the19th centuries, most of the countries in the region were colonized by Europeans. They have all now gained their independence.

Population explosion: people under pressure

China's population more than doubled in the late 18th century to reach over 400 million people by 1850. This enormous increase set millions of people on the move within China, in search of new farming land. It triggered rebellions and local wars between groups competing for scarce land and water resources. As local warlords built up private armies to fight one another, the authority of the Emperor in Peking began to collapse. The struggle for land was most fierce in the south-eastern, rice-growing provinces of Kwangtung and Fukien.

Merchant migration

Chinese merchants, especially from Fukien province, had a long history of trading with South-East Asia, or 'Nanyang', as the Chinese called it. Chinese trading communities existed in Vietnam, Thailand, the Philippines, Java, Sumatra, Malaya and Singapore.

By the 19th century many of these countries had been taken over by European powers. The Philippines had been colonized by the Spanish in the 16th century. The Dutch had settled at Batavia (Jakarta) on the island of Java in the 1610s and gradually absorbed Java and neighbouring islands into the Dutch East Indies. In competition, the British had established themselves on the Malayan peninsula and the island of Singapore. Later, in the 1880s, the French took over Vietnam and the British conquered all of Burma.

The Chinese merchants who had settled in these countries had a lot of trading experience. They were eager to do business with the new European rulers. The merchants became the middlemen, purchasing rice, pepper, coffee, indigo and other produce from the local farmers and selling them on to the Europeans to be exported overseas.

▲ Rice is the main crop of southern China and much of South-East Asia. These Vietnamese peasants sow and harvest their rice crop by hand.

▼ Chinese junks may look fragile, but for centuries they have sailed all around Asia.

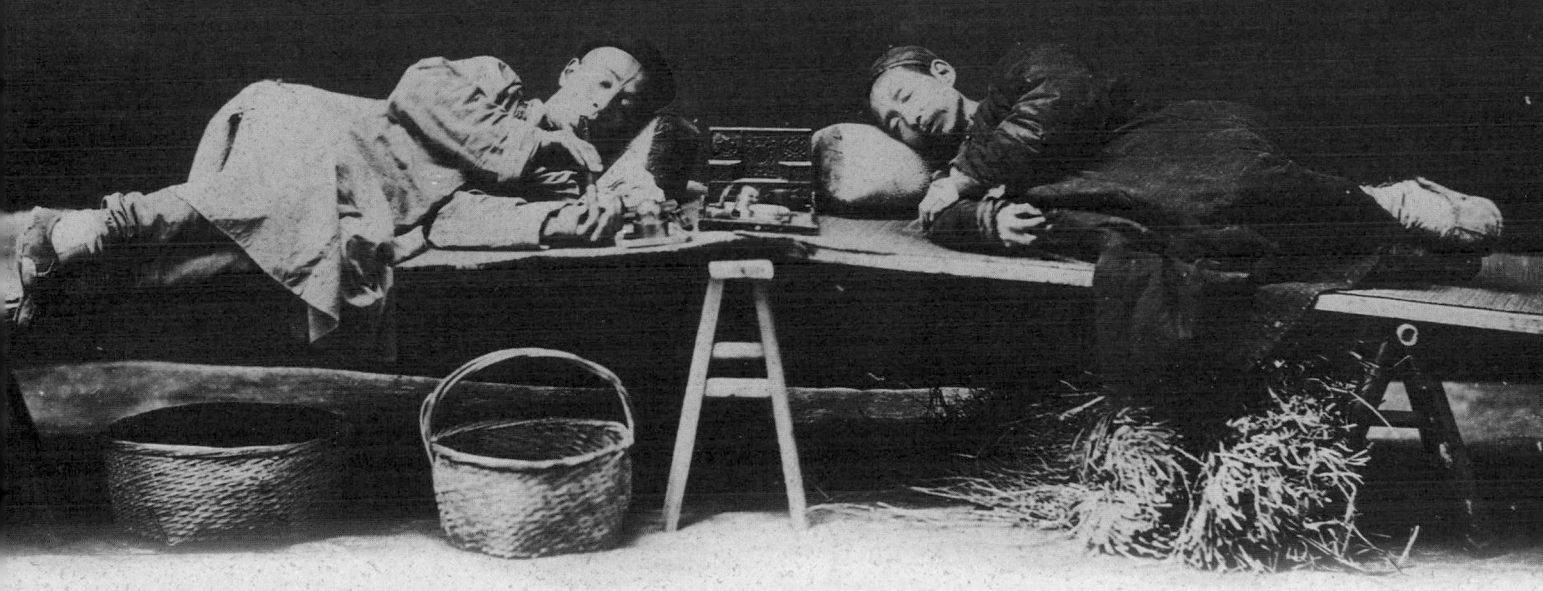

▲ People who became addicted to smoking opium often lost their will to work. The Chinese government accused the Europeans who imported opium into China of ruining its people.

▼ China was not strong enough to keep out foreigners. By 1850, the Americans, British, Dutch and French each had their own trading houses in the port of Canton.

European inroads into China

While Chinese merchants were settling in South-East Asia, all around China's coastline western merchants and missionaries were nibbling at China's independence. The British, French, Russians, Germans and Americans all wanted to trade freely with China. In particular, the British wanted to sell more of the drug opium to the Chinese. Money from the opium sales enabled them to buy Chinese tea to sell in Europe.

The Chinese government resisted them fiercely, but unfortunately for China the foreigners had better weapons and ships. From 1839-42, the British fought and won a coastal war which forced China to open up several important ports, including Canton, Amoy and Shanghai, to foreign trade. Britain also acquired the island of Hong Kong as a colony.

Humiliated by the 'British barbarians', the Chinese government still hoped to limit foreign influence by banning emigration. But as news filtered through of the riches to be had in other countries, more and more Chinese people decided to risk the Emperor's anger and seek work abroad.

7

The Chinese coolie trade

In theory the coolies had volunteered to work overseas for three years in return for a fixed wage. The reality, however, was different.

On the sugar-cane estates of Trinidad, Cuba, and Hawaii, Asian coolie labourers were guarded by overseers on horseback to ensure that they did not stop working.

The "Pig Trade"

There was a ready market for unskilled Chinese laborers, known as coolies, overseas. The coolie trade was brutal and violent. Locally, it was called the 'pig trade'. In theory the coolies had volunteered to work overseas for three years in return for a fixed wage. The reality, however, was different. Port cities like Canton always had a pool of hungry men looking for work. They were easy pickings for the labor recruiters. Many Chinese were lured into the dockside warehouses with false promises of good wages. Others were simply kidnapped from the streets. On board the ship, the conditions were so bad that often over half of the coolies died before they reached their destination.

Dangerous Work

On arrival, conditions were not much better. Labor on sugar plantations and in silver and gold mines was exhausting and dangerous. Hundreds of miners were killed when hastily dug tunnels collapsed or flooded. Moreover, the coolies' employers had endless excuses for cutting their wages, so that at the end of their contracts few had any savings. Many stayed on, hoping to earn money to take back home. These hardy survivors formed tiny Chinese communities in such far-flung places as Peru, Brazil, Trinidad, and Cuba.

The Chinese resented the cruel trade. In Canton crowds of angry people seized and murdered labor recruiters. In the 1860s the British persuaded the governor of Canton to establish a system of licensed labor emigration, with official inspections of coolie warehouses and ships, and proper contracts for the workers.

Coolies in Southeast Asia

Regulated labor emigration from China continued until 1914. From about 1875, most of the coolies went to British Malaya and the Dutch East Indies where they worked in tin mines and on rubber plantations. Some coolies also went to South Africa to work on the railroads.

▲ The tin industry in 19th-century Sumatra relied upon Chinese workers, such as these men smelting tin-ore into metal bars.

▼ This Chinese labourer from 1912 is a mobile tea shop. He is on his way to provide tea and snacks to fellow Chinese workers on a plantation in Hawaii.

The Chinese merchants who had settled in Malaya were often members of a lineage – a tight-knit organization of families who can trace their history back to a single male ancestor. There was a shortage of miners in Malaya, and the merchants soon realized that they could hire poor men from their lineages to work the tin-mines. The merchants were not careful about their workers' health, but they were able to provide them with a 'home-from-home'. They set up shops to sell them Chinese food, posted their wages back to their families in China, and established gambling and opium clubs to keep them entertained. No one else could command such a big workforce. Over 5 million Chinese labourers went to Malaya before 1900. Another 12 million arrived between 1900 and 1940. By the 1890s, Chinese businessmen controlled nearly all of Malaya's tin mines.

Not all of the coolies returned home at the end of their contracts. Some stayed behind and opened small grocery stores. By 1914, the permanent Chinese population of Malaya was 1.7 million. The Dutch East Indies had about 1 million Chinese residents.

Separate lives

In Malaya and the Dutch East Indies most of the population was Muslim. The Muslims and the Chinese did not marry one another or eat together. Under European rule, most towns had a European quarter, a Chinese quarter and a 'native' quarter, where the locals lived. The Chinese provided their own Chinese-language schools, shops and banks. In Malaya, the British government set up a Chinese Protectorate to control matters of Chinese immigration, labour welfare and education. This separate administration increased the isolation of the Chinese from the majority Muslim population of Malays.

The gold rush

As stories of magnificent wealth reached China, thousands of young men decided to try their luck in the Californian goldfields.

In the 1840s, gold was discovered in the USA. As stories of magnificent wealth reached China, thousands of young men decided to try their luck in the Californian goldfields. Like the coolies, most were from poor peasant families in Kwangtung province. None of the gold-seekers expected to be away forever – their plan was to return to Canton in a few years with money for their lineage to invest in land.

On the gold trail

Once in California, however, their hopes were dashed. The Chinese reached the goldfields after the best claims had been exhausted. The white miners barred them from the richest mines, forcing them to work valleys that had already been mined once, where the remaining gold was thinly spread and difficult to get at. Few miners made the fortune that would have allowed them to return home with pride.

In the 1850s, news that gold had been discovered in Australia offered fresh hope. Thousands of Chinese travelled there from California and more arrived direct from Canton until, by the early 1860s, there were over 55,000 Chinese in Australia. But there, as in California, they arrived after the best claims were already staked out. Sadly, the story was repeated again when gold was discovered in New Zealand in the 1860s.

Violence on the goldfields

Life on the goldfields was rough and dirty. The miners lived in tents and makeshift huts which flooded in the winter and were baking hot in the summer, and thefts and drunken fights between the men were common. Among the crowds of miners, the Chinese stood out with their different physical appearance. They were the butt of many racist taunts, and their hairstyle, a long plait or queue, was often singled out for ridicule.

▲ New Chinese arrivals to America stood out from everybody else because of their different dress, food, and hairstyle.

Whenever the gold began to run out in an area, violence erupted against the Chinese as the frustrated miners looked for someone to blame. Chinese equipment and huts were destroyed and they themselves were beaten or killed. Often high taxes or licence fees were introduced in an attempt to drive them off the goldfields.

'Cantons' – Chinese settlements in the goldfields

The Chinese survived by sticking together in their clans and building self-contained settlements known as 'Cantons'. In every goldfield, a Chinese merchant would set up shop, providing his countrymen with stores and postal and banking services. Most of the miners could not read or write, so the shopkeeper would write letters for them to their families, and read the news out loud from Chinese papers. He often supervised religious matters – most importantly, arranging the return of bodies of dead miners to China to be buried alongside their ancestors.

The shopkeeper also offered loans to his customers when their money ran out. This meant that soon many miners were in debt to their shopkeeper. In China, gambling was a normal pastime for men. Away from home, the lonely miners often spent far too much money on the games of Fan-tan and Pak-ah-pu and also on opium smoking. In spite of their difficulties, however, they remained hopeful. One miner in Oropuki in New Zealand spelled out his dreams in a slogan painted on his hut:

Peace: returning rich to our native Empire
Harmony: living joyfully together in this foreign state

A WORD OF CAUTION TO OUR FRIENDS, THE CIGAR-MAKERS.
Through the smoke it is easy to see the approach of Chinese cheap labor.

▼ Gold-mining brought riches to towns like Ballarat in Australia, but often Chinese miners were not allowed to share in the boom.

▲ White American workers warned employers, like the cigar-maker shown in this cartoon, not to hire cheap Chinese workers.

▲ As their money ran out, many Chinese miners turned to other trades like market gardening and vegetable selling.

▼ Anti-Chinese feeling sometimes turned violent. In 1880 rioters terrorized the Chinese residents of Denver, Colorado, and destroyed their houses and shops.

Beyond the gold-mines

Gradually, as their hopes of striking it rich in the goldfields faded, the Chinese looked for other employment. In the USA in the 1860s, 25,000 Chinese men worked on the railroads. The Chinese also moved into small businesses, such as restaurants, laundries and tailoring. They spread along the west coast of the USA and Canada, working in orchards, lumber-yards, fisheries and canneries. They also worked on the pineapple and sugar plantations of Hawaii. Inland, they worked in the coal and borax mines of Oregon, Wyoming, Utah and Nevada.

In Australia the former miners shifted into the cities of Sydney and Melbourne where they set up laundries and furniture-making shops. They also ran fruit and vegetable shops. In New Zealand most of the surviving miners became market gardeners.

The 'Yellow Peril'

Even though only a few of the goldseekers had been successful, to poor people in China the West still promised unlimited riches. Men from the Kwangtung province continued to emigrate until, by 1880, about 25 per cent of the workforce in California was Chinese. But Chinese immigration to the USA, Canada, Australia and New Zealand was fiercely opposed by racist groups and labour organizations who did not want Asians or Africans to share in their wealth. They called the Chinese, along with the Japanese and Koreans, the 'Yellow Peril'. This anti-Chinese feeling often erupted into violence. In 1880 anti-Chinese demonstrators destroyed the Chinese community in Denver, Colorado.

Chinatowns

The hostility of the whites encouraged the Chinese immigrants to live closely together, forming Chinatowns in cities like San Francisco, Vancouver, Melbourne and Sydney. By living in Chinatowns, the immigrants could use their own language, eat familiar foods, and play

Fan-tan and Pak-ah-pu. They often used lineage connections (see p. 9) to get work with Chinese merchants, making shoes, clothing and cigars.

Whites only

Eventually anti-Chinese protesters triumphed and governments in the USA, Canada, Australia and New Zealand stopped Chinese immigration. From the 1900s until at least the 1960s these countries maintained a whites-only immigration policy.

The US government first enacted a Chinese Exclusion Act in 1882. From 1904 onwards only the relatives of Chinese people born in the USA were allowed to enter the country. In Australia, the government invented a complicated literacy test which kept out anyone who could not read and write in English. New Zealand introduced poll taxes which were so high that they discouraged all but the wealthiest Chinese merchants from entering the country.

Shrinking communities

The anti-Chinese laws had the effect of making the Chinese communities even more isolated. Few Chinese men could now hope to bring their wives or children into their new country, and the Chinatowns turned into communities of ageing men. Even for those few families who were reunited in their new country, the dream of returning to Canton remained alive. The new countries still did not feel like home.

THE CHINESE

I HEREBY CONVENE A PUBLIC

MEETING

Of the inhabitants of the Borough, miners, and settlers of the Western District, to be held at the

TOWN HALL,

ON

SATURDAY, JUNE 4TH, 1881

At 8.30 p.m., to consider the best means to adopt to check the influx of the Chinese.

T. DANIEL, Mayor.

Burns, Printers, Western Star Office, Riverton.

▲ In New Zealand, as elsewhere, public meetings were held to discuss the 'Chinese problem' and to plan ways of driving the Chinese off the gold-fields.

Chinese women who emigrated tried to preserve their culture overseas. ▶ This bride, called Greta Fong, had a traditional Chinese wedding ceremony in the USA in 1927.

Filipino emigration to the USA

'Filipinos and dogs not allowed'.

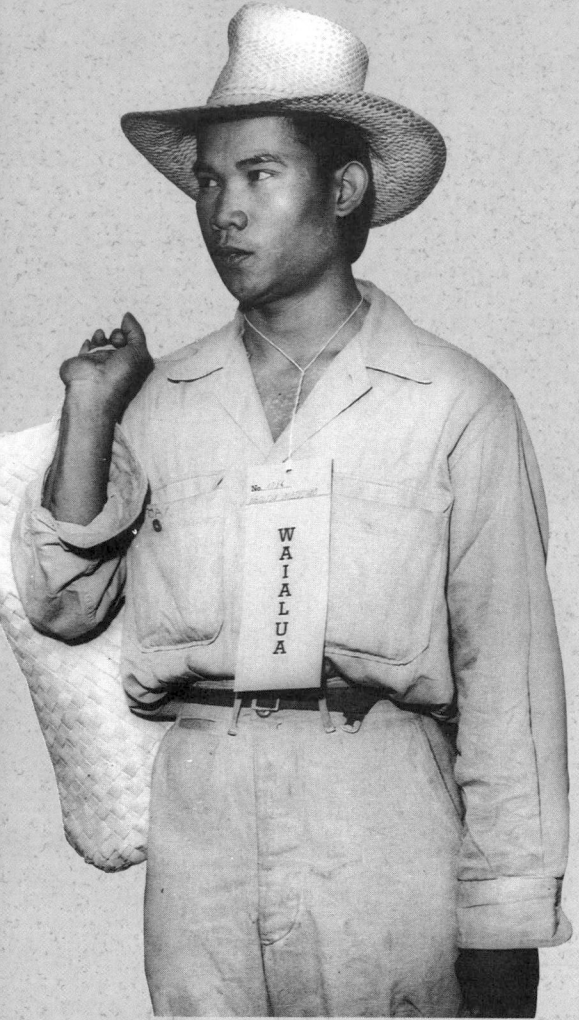

At first the Filipinos were the one group of Asians not covered by the United States' ban on Asian immigration. Spain had ruled the Philippines since the 16th century, but in 1898 the USA took over the islands. When, only a few years later, Chinese and Japanese workers were banned from entering the USA, American farmers began to import Filipino labourers. Because the Philippines were ruled by the USA, Filipinos were classified as American nationals and were not affected by the anti-Asian laws.

Plantation labourers

In 1906 a representative of the Hawaiian Sugar Planters' Association travelled to the Philippines in search of labourers. He signed up 300 men to work for three years on sugar plantations in Hawaii. Most were tenant farmers who did not have enough good quality land to farm at home. This first batch of workers was quickly followed by others. By 1930 there were over 100,000 Filipinos working in Hawaii and on the American mainland.

Hard work and bitter prejudice

Most of the Filipinos who went to Hawaii worked on one plantation only, but those on the mainland shifted around from job to job. In the winter they took jobs in cities as hotel janitors, chauffeurs and gardeners, but each summer they returned to the farms of the west coast to harvest strawberries, tomatoes, lettuce, asparagus, sugar beets and citrus fruits. Because they worked for very low wages they were often attacked by resentful white workers, especially during the Great Depression of 1929-34 when unemployment was high. Often lonely and cut off from the rest of society, Filipinos would get together with men from their home villages for fiestas of dancing, gambling and cock-fights. White Americans disapproved of these fiestas and looked down on the

▲ Filipino men recruited to work on Hawaii's pineapple and sugar plantations were labelled with the name of the plantation they were to be sent to.

Filipino women ▶ often worked in the pineapple canneries of Hawaii and California.

This plant scientist is typical of the new generation of Filipinos who were welcomed to the USA after the 1960s because of their education and professional skills.

Filipinos as lazy drunkards. Department stores and restaurants often displayed signs reading 'Filipinos and dogs not allowed'.

In 1934, after years of protest by labour unions and racist groups, the US government finally banned Filipino immigration. Thereafter the Filipino population dwindled until after the Second World War.

A new class of professional immigrants

After 1966 when the USA began to select immigrants for their professional qualifications rather than their race, educated Filipinos were in a good position to apply for entry. Many had been educated in the American-style colleges which the US government had built in the Philippines before independence. From the late 1960s, thousands of Filipino doctors, dentists, nurses and teachers moved to the USA. By 1990 over 1.5 million Filipinos had settled there.

The Philippines remains one of the poorest countries in Asia. Many Filipinos today still dream of leaving the crowded, polluted streets of Manila for a better life in the USA.

At first, many could not get their qualifications recognized by local employers and they had to take menial jobs at low wages, but by the mid-1980s the Filipinos enjoyed a high standard of living. The Filipino communities on the west coast of the USA and in Hawaii are still strong, but many of the new immigrants settled in eastern cities such as New York and Chicago. In New York alone, there are over 20,000 Filipino nurses. Over half of the driving instructors in Manhattan are Filipinos.

Communism and nationalism

Mao was backed by millions of peasants who had suffered a lifetime of poverty and hardship.

The Second World War, 1939-45, heralded the end of European and Japanese colonialism in Asia. After the war, the French in Indo-China, the Dutch in the Dutch East Indies, and the British in Burma and Malaya all handed over power to new, independent governments. Japan gave up its colony of Korea and also China which it had invaded during the war.

Some of the new governments that came to power after the war were communist ones. Communism tries to even out the differences between rich and poor people; it is opposed to individuals accumulating private wealth. To achieve this, communist governments take over (or nationalize) all private property and try to administer the country's wealth so that everyone has equal access to education, housing and jobs.

The communist revolution

In China, in 1949, Chairman Mao Tse-tung led the communists to victory after a bitter civil war. Mao was backed by millions of peasants who had suffered a lifetime of poverty and hardship. Only the island of Taiwan resisted the communists; it became a haven for the Chinese who opposed communism.

Chairman Mao, leader of the Chinese Communist Party, promised to bring wealth and modern technology to China's millions of poverty-stricken peasants. This Communist Party poster shows Mao as a big, strong leader, backed by well-dressed and happy workers.

The communists' triumph was a turning point for the overseas Chinese. Even after two or three generations abroad, many families had still dreamed of returning permanently to China. 1949 was the year when many finally accepted that their emigration was permanent.

A warmer welcome from the West

The Chinese in North America and Australasia were helped by the increasingly friendly attitude of their host countries. During the Japanese occupation of China, sympathetic western governments had allowed wives and children to come from China to join their male relatives abroad. Also, during the war some Chinese men had fought in the armies of the USA, Canada, Australia and New Zealand. This act of loyalty to their host countries weakened the common prejudice that the Chinese only looked after their own interests.

During the 1960s and 1970s the governments of the USA, Canada, Australia and New Zealand abolished their whites-only immigration policies. Now skilled and professional workers from China were welcomed as useful immigrants. The USA alone accepted 160,000 Chinese immigrants in the 1960s and 1970s. They came from all parts of the mainland, Taiwan and also the British colony of Hong Kong. By the mid-1990s, 1.5 million Chinese lived in the USA.

▲ The Red Army was the army of the Chinese Communist Party. It was made up of thousands of peasants who wanted to share out rich people's property between everyone. After the Red Army's victory in 1949, many overseas Chinese were too frightened to return to China in case they had to give their property to the Communists.

◄ This Chinese family in Melbourne, Australia is one of the many which have achieved success overseas since Western governments began to welcome skilled Asian immigrants in the 1960s.

Nationalism in Indonesia

While the Chinese were finally getting a friendly reception in North America, Australasia and Britain, Chinese residents in South-East Asia faced a more uncertain future. Indonesia, which won its independence from the Dutch in 1950, soon showed that the Chinese were no longer welcome.

Indonesia is made up of many different islands and peoples. The new government tried to build a sense of national identity amongst them by creating a national language and highlighting things that most Indonesians had in common, such as Islam. With a different language, religion and physical appearance, Indonesia's 2 million Chinese did not fit in to this new image of Indonesian nationality. Moreover, they were disliked because of their success in business and their old reputation as supporters of the Dutch.

In 1959, the government forced the closure of thousands of Chinese shops, newspapers, and schools. The government's open hostility to the Chinese often encouraged ordinary Indonesians to attack them. In 1968, for example, 100 Chinese were killed in a pogrom in West Borneo.

Since the 1960s, many Chinese have only been able to survive in Indonesia by abandoning the things that make them Chinese: their language, religion, family loyalties, and sometimes even their Chinese names.

On the move again

As anti-Chinese feeling grew, the Chinese began to emigrate again, often to the island state of Singapore. Singapore welcomed the Chinese and has thrived on their business skills to become one of the financial capitals of the East.

In Malaysia, the Chinese have suffered a similar fate, especially in recent years as the government has stressed Islam as the most important part of Malaysian nationality. Some Chinese have emigrated from Malaysia to Australia.

Singapore welcomed the Chinese. Ancient traditions such as dragon-making still thrive in Singapore's Chinatown, which nestles amongst modern tower blocks.

Emigration of the 'Indonesian Dutch'

The Chinese were not the only people displaced from Indonesia. During the 1950s, 150,000 ethnic Indonesians and whites born and brought up in the country left Indonesia to settle in the Netherlands. They emigrated because they had worked for the colonial government or army, and they were worried that they would be persecuted for their connections with the Dutch.

The Netherlands spent millions of gilders on housing, education and employment training for the immigrants and the Dutch people welcomed them as refugees from their old colony. Even with such goodwill, however, many of the immigrants found it difficult to settle. After the tropical splendour of Indonesia, the climate was harsh, the houses and gardens seemed tiny and Dutch social life appeared frighteningly formal. The Indonesians often viewed the Dutch as aloof, whereas the Dutch often saw the Indonesians as lazy and untidy spendthrifts.

Despite the difficulties, most of the immigrants were able to find work, although many had to take clerical or manual jobs below the level of their experience. Some, noticing the willingness of the Dutch to try new foods, opened restaurants all over the country specializing in Indonesian and Malay dishes.

Indonesian and Malay food quickly became popular throughout the Netherlands.

Vietnam, Laos and Cambodia

Thousands clambered into small boats and floated out into the South China Sea

▲ French styles of building in Vietnam survive as a reminder of the country's colonial past.

▼ By the 1970s the Vietnam War had devastated the country.

Exodus from Indo-China

During the Second World War, the French had lost control of their old colony Indo-China and, in 1945, communists seized power in North Vietnam. After the war, the French regained power in the south but they were unable to crush the communists. In 1954, they pulled out of the area, having first divided Indo-China into the independent countries of Vietnam, Cambodia and Laos. Before leaving, they set up a non-communist government in South Vietnam.

After the French had gone, the USA began to supply South Vietnam with soldiers and weapons to protect it from the communists. Gradually the Americans became embroiled in a long and bloody war in Vietnam and also in neighbouring Laos and Cambodia. Australia too joined in this war. But they were unable to halt the communist advance, especially as many poor peasants supported the communists. In April 1975, Saigon, the capital of South Vietnam, was captured by the communists. Soon afterwards, the pro-American governments in Cambodia and Laos also collapsed.

The first refugees, 1975-76

After the fall of Saigon, Vietnamese who had worked for either the South Vietnamese government or the Americans feared persecution by the communists if they remained in Vietnam. Thousands clambered into small boats and floated out into the South China Sea where they were picked up by American ships. From Laos, over 160,000 people fled across the border to Thailand.

This first wave of refugees went to either the USA or France. They were often wealthy and highly educated, literate in both French and English. Many were Roman Catholics, the descendants of Buddhists who had been converted to Christianity by French missionaries. Some had visited the USA or France as students. Their skills and knowledge of western culture eased their arrival in the USA and France.

The boat people

In 1977, a new wave of middle-class refugees began. Thousands of business people, shopkeepers, landlords, doctors, and schoolteachers, frightened of the communists, tried to leave Vietnam. They crowded into ramshackle fishing boats and set sail on the open sea in the hope of finding a friendly country to land in. The boat people risked starvation, storms and attack by pirates and sharks, but still they kept on leaving. Hundreds died at sea, but hundreds of thousands ended up in refugee camps in Malaysia, Hong Kong, the Philippines and Indonesia.

As the business executives fled Vietnam, transport and shopping systems collapsed, causing food shortages, unemployment and price rises. It was a vicious cycle: the collapsing economy encouraged yet more people to leave and made it harder still for the communists to create a stable, prosperous country.

At the same time, across the border in Cambodia, thousands of Khmers fled into Thailand to escape the communist regime of Pol Pot, and the war which had broken out with Vietnam. Swamped by refugees, Thailand, Malaysia and Indonesia appealed to the world for help.

Settling the boat people

The USA accepted the largest number of refugees: almost 1 million by 1990. About 650,000 were from Vietnam; the remainder were Cambodians and Laotians. Many settled

▲ Desperate to leave war-torn Vietnam, thousands of refugees set sail for other countries in rickety fishing boats.

▼ Much of Cambodia's unique architecture and culture were destroyed in the war during the 1970s and 1980s.

in the west in California and Oregon and in the south in Texas and Oklahoma. Australia and Canada accepted 80,000 refugees each and France about 125,000. Germany and Britain also took some refugees.

A mixed reception

For many among this second wave of refugees, settling into their new countries was much harder. The Chinese from Indo-China were used to being a minority community and providing their own forms of self-help, such as Chinese-language classes and family employment networks. As refugees, they could use this experience to help them adjust to living in their new countries.

The Vietnamese, on the other hand, had never before been in a minority, cut off by language and culture from the bulk of the population. Few could speak a western language. They knew little about life in western countries.

▲ Frightened and homeless Cambodians fled to refugee camps in Thailand. Many remained there for years, praying for a country like Canada or Australia to offer them a new home.

▼ The refugees had to complete many forms and undergo several interviews with officials before being granted entry to a new country.

Language difficulties often stopped refugees from getting good jobs in their new countries, so many, like this man in Australia, opened shops which served other refugees.

In addition, by the late 1970s the economies of the host countries were in recession, with rising unemployment. The refugees were often accused by locals of stealing their jobs, or told that they were not proper refugees and were only looking for a better way of life rather than fleeing political persecution.

Rivalry over jobs and cultural misunderstanding were often expressed in racist graffiti, name-calling, and assaults. In Texas and California there were fights over jobs between Vietnamese and local fishermen. In Melbourne a clash occurred between white Australians and their Vietnamese neighbours who wanted to barbecue a dog in their backyard. A teenage girl at an American high-school describes a typical experience:

I was called 'fish breath' and it made me angry. I am not a 'chink' or a 'slant eye'. I do not like being called names and I know that most of my friends at school do not like it either.

A drop in status

For many of the refugees, learning a new language in adulthood has proved impossible. They have had to take factory jobs where they do not need to speak much. In Brisbane, Australia, a former vice-chancellor of a university in Saigon became a gardener in a cement factory. It was, he admitted, hard for him to accept his lowly position, but he was grateful to have a job and he took comfort from the fact that he was respected by both Australians and Vietnamese as a good community leader.

Little Saigon in Los Angeles is the meeting place for the city's Vietnamese population. The old people especially get together to talk about the friends and places they have left behind.

▲ **Little Saigon in Los Angeles provides a collection of shops, services, restaurants, temples, churches, and community clubs for the local Vietnamese community.**

▲ **Buddhism is central to the peoples of Indo-China. In their new countries many refugees have helped to build Buddhist temples to maintain their religion and their sense of community.**

Education: the key to the future

Many refugees look forward to regaining their former middle-class status through the achievements of their children, who have found it much easier to learn a new language. Eagerly supported by their parents, Indo-Chinese children often do well in school, especially in science subjects, maths and music.

While the children represent hope for the future, their experiences also bring out the stresses of adapting to a new culture. Indo-Chinese people value loyalty to the family and respect for elders. As their children experiment with part-time jobs, dating and modern fashions, many parents and grandparents worry that their traditional family life will collapse. A teenage boy in Oklahoma City explains some of the difficulties:

When I first got my job at McDonalds, I always gave my money to my father. When my American friends found out, they laughed. They thought that that was funny. Now I need my money for my car, and for my dating. I tried to tell my father that this is how we do it in America, but I don't think he understands. He still thinks we are in Vietnam.

Tet: the Vietnamese New Year

One of the most important festivals for Vietnamese people is Tet, the joyous celebration of the Vietnamese New Year. Tet is a time when ancestors are worshipped, old quarrels are healed, and families and friends get together to laugh and talk over old times.

Amongst the refugee communities, Tet is also a time for remembering the loss of their homeland. Tet is often held in the social clubs, Buddhist temples and Roman Catholic churches that the refugees have built as symbols of their new community. In amongst the dances and folk songs, the Vietnamese will remember the soldiers who died fighting against the communists. Often the South Vietnamese flag will be flown and there will be speeches condemning the communist government in Vietnam.

Opportunities for the future

Today cities like San Francisco, Vancouver and Sydney proudly celebrate their Chinese heritage.

▼ Chinatowns such as this one in San Francisco are lively and popular tourist attractions.

Asian professionals ▶ are now a highly valued part of the workforce in many western countries.

The Chinese communities in North America and Australasia have come a long way since the first goldseekers were abused and shunned by the locals. Today cities like San Francisco, Vancouver and Sydney proudly celebrate their Chinese heritage. Where once Chinatowns were viewed as dangerous and sinister, now they have become highly valued tourist attractions. Non-Chinese people visit Chinatowns to seek out Chinese food, Kung Fu classes, and ancient Chinese remedies like acupuncture.

The Chinese themselves are no longer confined to their old jobs as labourers and factory workers. Aided by education and the influx of skilled and professional Chinese workers after the 1960s, they have

▲ This car factory in Thailand needs a skilled workforce. Like many other Asian countries, Thailand does not want its skilled workers to emigrate to richer Western countries.

produced scientists, engineers, computer programmers, surgeons, pilots, lawyers and business executives. Australia's Chinese community in particular has been swelled by a steady flow of Chinese professionals emigrating from Indonesia and Malaysia where they no longer feel welcome.

Not all of the Chinese in western countries are successful professionals. In the USA the best-paid Chinese workers are those who have come from Taiwan or the urban part of Hong Kong, where the western-style education system makes them well qualified to fit into the American workforce. Immigrants from the Chinese mainland often lack these advantages. They are more likely to end up in low-paid factory jobs. Many women from mainland China work in the garment industry as sewing-machine operators.

The Chinese in Britain

Britain too now has a Chinese community, chiefly made up of people who came from the rural part of Hong Kong in the 1950s and 1960s to work in Chinese restaurants in the Soho district of London. By 1980, Britain's Chinese population had reached 150,000. Few have left the catering industry altogether, but some have emigrated for a second time to open restaurants in Scandinavia, Belgium, the Netherlands and Germany.

The restaurant workers have maintained strong links with Hong Kong and many families have sent their children back to their grandparents in Hong Kong to receive a Chinese education. In 1997, however, the British government returned Hong Kong to China. Many Hong Kong Chinese are uncertain

▲ Most of Britain's Chinese population works in the catering industry in restaurants like this one in London's Chinatown.

▲ In the 19th century Protestant missionaries converted many Koreans to Christianity. Today the Church is often an important community centre for Korean emigrants to the USA.

about the future under China's Communist government. For those who live in Britain, 1997 may have marked the time when their new country began to feel properly like home.

Emigration from Korea

Another new Asian community is that of the Koreans in the USA. Before 1910, several thousand Korean laborers had settled in Hawaii and California, but emigration to the USA stopped in the years when Japan ruled Korea (1910-45) and America had a whites-only immigration policy.

In 1966, when the USA abolished its ban on Asian immigration, many Koreans from South Korea were eager to try life there. About 300,000 entered in the 1960s and 1970s and by 1990 the Korean community totalled over 800,000. Most were middle-class professionals who expected to get skilled, well-paid jobs in their rich new country, but few could speak English and often their foreign qualifications were rejected by American employers. Many doctors and pharmacists had to take menial jobs such as cleaners, labourers, and factory-hands.

Frustrated, the Koreans created their own opportunities. In run-down inner-city neighbourhoods, especially in Los Angeles, they opened shops to cater to poor people. They worked long hours, but also ensured that they educated their children to the maximum level in the American education system. With success at university, the immigrants' children have been able to get jobs as scientists, doctors, and academics.

Emigration from South Korea continues today, mostly still to the USA. In addition, thousands of Koreans take contract jobs in the Middle East and on foreign ships, often earning twice what they could at home.

The tiger economies

The emigration of many of the people we have looked at in this book was caused by poverty or lack of opportunity. China, Korea, the Philippines, Vietnam — all seemed poor in comparison with the West. In the last two decades, however, the economies of these countries have begun to grow rapidly, so much so that they are called the 'tiger economies'. Where once skilled workers and businessmen sought opportunities abroad, today some of the emigrants are beginning to look back to the fresh opportunities at home. Expatriate Chinese businessmen have always been keen to invest money in the booming economies of Taiwan and Hong Kong. Now many are investing in mainland China as well.

◀ Shanghai's 'tiger economy' has attracted Chinese businessmen resident overseas to invest in its industrial and technological development.

After the wars

For the Cambodians, Laotians and Vietnamese, the mass exodus of their people has only just begun to ease. In Hong Kong there are still thousands of boat people who refuse to return to Vietnam but who can no longer find refuge in another country. After the years of warfare, the countries of Indo-China desperately need skilled workers, business executives and administrators to rebuild their economies. But the memories of war are often bitter ones. It will be a long time before many of the former refugees will be prepared to return home.

◀ This elaborately decorated gateway signals the entry to Chinatown in Manchester. Similar gateways exist in Chinatowns all over the world.

◀ In the 1990s few countries are still willing to accept Vietnamese refugees. These Vietnamese children are locked in refugee camps in Hong Kong. They will probably be forced to go back to Vietnam.

Timeline

AD 68	Buddhism reaches China from India and becomes one of the most important religions in Vietnam and Korea.
1290	The first Muslim countries are established in north Sumatra.
1511	The Portuguese conquer Malacca (Melaka). This is the beginning of 450 years of European dominance in South-East Asia.
late-1600s	Spain conquers the Philippines.
1619	The Dutch establish a trading base at Batavia (Jakarta) on the island of Java.
1641	The Dutch capture Malacca.
1786	The British occupy Penang.
1819	The British occupy Singapore.
1824	Anglo-Dutch Treaty divides the Malay world between the British and the Dutch.
1839-42	The Opium War. Britain acquires the island of Hong Kong as a colony.
1840s-60s	Gold-rush era. Thousands of men from Canton travel to the goldfields of California, Australia and New Zealand.
1856-60	Anglo-French war with China.
1859	Export of coolie labourers is brought under control and licensed by the Chinese governor of Canton.
1859	The French navy seizes Saigon. By 1884 France has taken over the whole of Vietnam.
1860s-80s	Chinese men migrate to the west coast of USA and Canada in search of work.
1880s	The USA, Canada, Australia and New Zealand begin to bring in restrictions on Chinese immigration.
1897	France establishes the Union of Indo-China.
1898	China leases 300 square miles of the mainland, next to Hong Kong, to Britain for 99 years.
1898	USA takes over the Philippines from Spain.
1910	Japan annexes Korea.
1912	Revolution in China.
1914-18	World War I.
1920s-30s	Nationalist and communist opposition to European rule begins to grow in South-East Asia. In China, Mao Tse-tung builds support for a communist revolution.
1934	The USA bans immigration from the Philippines.
1939-45	World War II.
1945	Vietnamese communists seize power in the north of Vietnam.
1945	Civil war breaks out in China between communists and anti-communists.
1948	The Republic of Korea is founded.
1949	Chairman Mao leads the Communist Red Army to victory in China's civil war. Anti-communists flee to Taiwan.
1950-53	The Korean War.
1953	Laos becomes independent from France. A long struggle begins between pro- and anti-communist Laotians.
1954	France leaves Vietnam. Communists are in power in the north of the country; the anti-communist government in the south is supported by the USA.
1957	The Malay states win independence.
1959	Indonesia suppresses Chinese-language education and newspapers; over 120,000 Chinese leave Indonesia.
1962-73	The USA, Canada, Australia and New Zealand stop discriminating against non-white immigrants.
1965	US troops enter South Vietnam to fight the communists.
1973	US troops pull out of Vietnam, but the USA continues to support the government of South Vietnam.
1975	North Vietnamese communists defeat the South Vietnamese government and capture Saigon. Vietnam is reunited under communist rule.
1975	Communists win power in Laos.
1975	In Cambodia, Pol Pot leads the communist Khmer Rouge to power.
1977	Vietnam invades Cambodia. Pol Pot is eventually defeated but his Khmer Rouge force remains powerful.
1977-85	Hundreds of thousands of 'boat people' flee economic and social collapse.
late-1980s	After 40 years of warfare, economic and social stability begins to return to Vietnam, Cambodia and Laos.
1988	South Korea hosts the Olympic Games.
1996	Vietnamese refugees in Hong Kong riot against being sent back to Vietnam.
1997	Britain returns Hong Kong to China.

Glossary

acupuncture: an ancient Chinese medical technique which involves puncturing special points of a person's body with fine needles to relieve pain and disease.

ancestor-worship: the tradition of honouring with special graves, ancestor-halls and regular ceremonies the memory of one's dead ancestors.

Australasia: the region covering Australia, New Zealand and the islands of the South Pacific.

borax: a white mineral often used as a cleansing agent, water softener, or preservative.

Buddhism: the religion based on the beliefs of Gautama Buddha (c. 563-483 BC), who taught that people can attain freedom from suffering if they give up their likes and dislikes and their love of material possessions.

claim: in mining, an area of land staked out by a miner as his own territory.

clan: in China, a group made up of all the people who have the same surname.

colony: a country or territory which has been taken over and is governed by another country.

Confucianism: the philosophy of Confucius (551-479 BC), followed by many Chinese, Koreans and Vietnamese, which stresses respect for one's superiors, modesty, virtue and proper behaviour.

commerce: the buying and selling of things, usually on a big scale.

coolie: an unskilled labourer, often expected to work for low wages.

emigrate: to leave one's country to settle permanently in another country.

exodus: a departure, usually of many people.

export: to sell goods and produce for use in foreign countries.

fiesta: a festivity or celebration.

haven: a place of safety or refuge.

immigrate: to arrive in a new country intending to stay permanently.

indigo: a dark blue powder used as a dye.

Indo-China: the region covering Vietnam, Laos and Cambodia.

Industrial Revolution: the period of rapid economic change in 18th and 19th-century Europe marked by the growth of factories and the use of machinery to manufacture products cheaply and in large numbers.

Islam: the religion which recognizes Allah as the true God and Muhammad as his prophet; it was founded by Muhammad in the 7th century AD.

junk: a type of boat with a flat bottom, used in the China seas.

Khmer: a member of the largest ethnic group in Cambodia; also the main language of Cambodia.

Khmer Rouge: the main communist party of Cambodia; translated, it means 'the Red Khmers'.

labour recruiter: someone who is paid to sign up or recruit people as contract labourers.

lineage: in China, a tight-knit organization of families who can trace their history back to a single male ancestor, often from many generations ago; pronounced lin-ee-uj.

malaria: a persistent fever, sometimes fatal, caused by a parasite in the bloodstream which is spread between humans by the bite of mosquitos.

missionary: a religious person, often a Christian, who attempts to convince other people to adopt his or her religious beliefs.

mosque: a muslim place of worship.

Muslim: a follower of Islam.

nationalization: a policy whereby a government takes over private property (such as a railway company) and administers it so that its benefits and profits are available for all the people in the country, not just the former owners of the property.

opium: an addictive drug extracted from the seed pod of the opium poppy.

persecution: the persistent attacking or harassment of someone, especially because of their race, religion, or political beliefs.

plantation: an estate or a large farm on which crops such as sugar, rubber, and coffee are grown.

pogrom: an organized massacre (mass killing), especially of people of belonging to an ethnic or religious minority.

porcelain: a hard, fine quality ceramic or pottery used for dinner plates; often called 'china'.

prejudice: an opinion against someone or something which has been made without knowing anything about that person or subject.

refugee: someone who is fleeing danger; someone who is forced out of their home territory by war, famine or political violence.

Roman Catholic: a Christian who recognizes the Pope as God's representative on earth. Roman Catholics accept the Pope's teachings and interpretations of the Bible as God's truth.

smelting: the process of fusing or melting something in order to extract the metal inside.

warlord: in China, a powerful man who controlled land, money and his own private army.

Index